GOOD BONES

Good Bones

MAGGIE
SMITH

T|P

TUPELO PRESS
North Adams, Massachusetts

Library of Congress Cataloging-in-Publication Data
Names: Smith, Maggie, 1977- author. Title: Good bones / Maggie Smith.
Description: First edition. | North Adams, Massachusetts : Tupelo Press, [2017]
Identifiers: LCCN 2017026607 | ISBN 9781946482013 (pbk. original : alk. paper)
Subjects: LCSH: Motherhood--Poetry.
Classification: LCC PS3619.M5918 A6 2017 | DDC 811/.6--dc23
International edition ISBN 978-1-946482-08-2

Cover and text designed and composed in Adobe Jenson by Josef Beery.
Cover photo by Steve McSweeney, iStock Photo.

First edition: October 2017.

This book's epigraph is an excerpt of two lines from "Impressionism" from
From the New World: Poems 1976–2014 by Jorie Graham.
Copyright © 2015 Jorie Graham. Reprinted by permission of HarperCollins Publishers.

The epigraph for "Your Tongue" is an excerpt from Aracelis Girmay's
"St. Elizabeth," from the book *Kingdom Animalia*. Copyright © 2011 Aracelis Girmay.
Reprinted with permission of The Permissions Company, Inc., on behalf of
BOA Editions, Ltd. (www.boaeditions.org).

The poem "Poem with a line from *Bluets*" features an excerpt from Maggie Nelson's
book *Bluets*. Copyright © 2009 by Maggie Nelson. Reprinted with the permission of
Wave Books, www.wavepoetry.com.

Tupelo Press
P.O. Box 1767, North Adams, Massachusetts 01247
(413) 664–9611 / editor@tupelopress.org / www.tupelopress.org

Tupelo Press is an award-winning independent literary press that publishes fine fiction,
nonfiction, and poetry in books that are a joy to hold as well as read.
Tupelo Press is a registered 501(c)(3) nonprofit organization, and we rely on public
support to carry out our mission of publishing extraordinary work that may be outside
the realm of the large commercial publishers. Financial donations are welcome and are
tax deductible.

Publication of this book has been made possible by a generous contribution in honor of
Rosie, Lena, Julia, and Marie Jacob, and mothers everywhere.

There's no way back believe me.
I'm writing you from there.
—Jorie Graham

Contents

~

Weep Up

It's only technically morning. Not even the birds believe it.
From her crib, my daughter tries to wake them, saying *weep* for *wake*.
Weep up, birds. What else could silence mean to her but sleep?
We might be the first awake on our street, the neighbors' breathing still
regular and slow, all the porches lit and moths losing their minds
in that light. Rising, spellbound in the blurry dawn, I become my mother.
Twentieth-century sunrise was just like this—sad, soft-focus
ocher like an overexposed Polaroid. The sun is just now brimming
over the golden edge of the lawn, and dew begins to sizzle there.
In the dark I hear *weep up, weep up, birds,* until they do.

First Fall

I'm your guide here. In the evening-dark
morning streets, I point and name.
Look, the sycamores, their mottled,
paint-by-number bark. Look, the leaves
rusting and crisping at the edges.
I walk through Schiller Park with you
on my chest. Stars smolder well
into daylight. Look, the pond, the ducks,
the dogs paddling after their prized sticks.
Fall is when the only things you know
because I've named them
begin to end. Soon I'll have another
season to offer you: frost soft
on the window and a porthole
sighed there, ice sleeving the bare
gray branches. The first time you see
something die, you won't know it might
come back. I'm desperate for you
to love the world because I brought you here.

MARKED

They are alone, the woman and the girl.
The man has gone over the mountain

to work for a year, maybe longer, and the sunlight
here is a little bitter, the color of turmeric,

the same gold as the leaves floating down.
The girl has an eye like a spyglass for birds.

She must be marked, the woman thinks.
Wherever she walks, the shadow of a hawk

falls on her, the way a light trains on something.
In this thick forest, light can't touch

every leaf, but the woman watches
wind touch all of them. If they weren't paper-

thin, this rustling would be a hammering
like hooves on hard ground. The man will return,

but what a strange homecoming to the world
belonging to the woman and child. They cut

its intricate shapes from nothing, like silhouettes
from paper. They have a rhythm. Mornings

to the creek on horseback, ocher leaves
falling through ocher air nearly indistinguishable.

Evenings, at the fire, telling stories the man
won't know. Maybe there is something about

his hands, rough as bark, the girl will remember.
But if she's grown wild in this wilderness,

who could blame her. Once small enough
to fit inside the hawk's fallen shadow,

now she can almost outrun it, the dark
blade of a wingtip scissoring across her face.

SKY

Why is the sky so tall and over everything?

What you draw as a blue stripe high above
a green stripe, white-interrupted, the real sky
starts at the tip of each blade of grass and goes
up, up, as far as you can see. Our house stops
at the roof, at the glitter-black overlap of shingles
where the sky presses down, bearing the weight
of space, dark and sparkling, on its back.
Think of sky not as blue, not as over,
but as the invisible surround, a soft suit
you wear close to the skin. When you walk,
the soles of your feet take turns on the ground,
but the rest of you is in the sky, enveloped in sky.
As you move through it, you make a tunnel
in the precise size and shape of your body.

This Town

You might tell yourself you want to leave. Hell,
you might want to leave. This town, this stinking town,

the woods and cornfields that lured you from home
late at night while your parents slept, bulldozed

for strip malls and surface parking. Once you could lie
in the tall grass with the boy you loved, the deer

just feet away, and never be found. You haven't been
kissed like that in years, pressed to the earth in a place

you called nowhere because there was nothing
to fence in. You might have dreamt it except for

the details: the taste of drugstore wine, the speckled
fawn staring, not even flicking an ear. Acorns

pinged a barn roof and rolled in the gutters
like arcade pinballs. Bats darted at the treeline,

half-drunk, hungry for your hair. Face it, your life
is not what it was. The boy you loved is a dozen

years behind you, whatever that translates to in miles.
He's married to someone else and has a daughter,

and so do you. His parents don't live in the house
you crept to, the house in the sticks. Teenagers now

can't have what you had in this town—nowheres
all along Old 3-C highway, hawks appearing wherever

you went like a talisman, the crickets in stereo,
tricking you into believing they had you surrounded.

But the creek still runs cold behind the house
where your parents raised you, where they live,

and the deer still find their way to the backyard
somehow, deep in the suburbs. They materialize

behind the house and just as quickly, they're gone.

TWENTIETH CENTURY

I must have missed the last train out of this gray city.
I'm scrolling the radio through *shhhhh*. The streetlamps

fill with light, right on time, but no one is pouring it in.
Twentieth Century, you're gone. You're tucked into

a sleeping car, rolling to god-knows-where, and I'm
lonely for you. I know it's naïve. But your horrors

were far away, and I thought I could stand them.
Twentieth Century, we had a good life more or less,

didn't we? You made me. You wove the long braid
down my back. You kissed me in the snowy street

with everyone watching. You opened your mouth a little
and it scared me. Twentieth Century, it's *me*, it's *me*.

You said that to me once, as if I'd forgotten your face.
You strung me out until trees seemed to breathe,

expanding and contracting. You played "American Girl"
and turned it up loud. You said I was untouchable.

Do you remember the nights at Alum Creek, the lit
windows painting yellow Rothkos on the water?

Are they still there, or did you take them with you?
Say something. I'm here, waiting, scrolling the radio.

On every frequency, someone hushes me. Is it you?
Twentieth Century, are you there? I thought you were

a simpler time. I thought we'd live on a mountain
together, drinking melted snow, carving hawk totems

from downed pines. We'd never come back. Twentieth
Century, I was in so deep, I couldn't see an end to you.

THE HAWK

The hawk has never seen a girl.
This new creature—smaller than a fawn,

song unlike a bird's—hushes the air
with her gold hair. The clearing seems

an invitation to light her, but the hawk
has no light to shine, only shadow.

He hovers, training his own dark double
on the girl. They are tethered, an invisible

string between them. She rarely speaks
but sings. The hawk has never seen notes

shaped like hers, each one an empty
locket with space inside it, but for what?

This is not for birds to understand.
The hawk loves the girl best

in the open, only sunlight strumming
the tether between them, her notes

rising easily to him the way an echo
homes to the voice that calls it.

LONDON PLANE

The plane tree peels
to yellowed newsprint,

littering the yard
with stiff sleeves of bark

collaged ivory and dove.
A gray squirrel stands

on its hind legs, gently
combing clover

with its paws, as if
it were fur on the back

of some animal it loves
and tends to.

Of everywhere
I've lived, this is home

because my daughter
draws it: periwinkle

crayon for the peeling
shake siding, black

pluses for windows,
a handful of pastels

for the plane tree,
pale and painterly.

Every year it sheds
its skin down to white bone.

I pick up a mottled cuff
and cup my wrist

to show my daughter
how to wear it.

Accidental Pastoral

I must have just missed a parade—
horse droppings and hard candy
in the road, miniature American
flags staked into the grass, plastic
chairs lining the curb down this

two-lane highway, 36 in the open
country, briefly Main Street in town.
When I was small, I sat on a curb
only a dozen miles from here, my feet
in the ashtray-dirty gutter, and watched

stars-and-stripes girls wheeling
their batons, slicing the sun-dumb
air into streamers. I can still hear
the click of cellophaned candies
on pavement. I didn't want to

leave town, not then, and I never left.
I am not a parade, my one car passing
through Centerburg, Ohio, too late.
The chairs are empty. The children
are unwrapping golden butterscotches

in the cool, shuttered houses.
But look up—the clouds are stories
tall, painted above Webb's Marathon,
and flat-bottomed as if resting on something
they push against though it holds them.

Museum

In the circa 1983 wood-paneled museum
        of the family we were then, stoppered

                like a bottle now, smelling of Salem
                    menthols and Naugahyde

potatoes split open in the pot roast,
        the couch was burgundy with birds

                and over it, stocking-capped children
                  skated on a frozen pond

in an oil painting, scarves flying behind them.
        In the veneer of 1983, the picture window

                made a picture of the backyard hill
                  sloping toward the creek

at the bottom of the canvas, if the window
        had been a canvas and painted there

                were ash trees, one buckeye
                  waiting for its spiky jewels.

Smoke must have risen from our chimney
      though we saw only fire. In the museum

          where we lived, a spoon drew circles
            inside a saucepan, ringing

like a zen bell where my mother stood forever
      at the stove, an installation, or was it

          my mother who rang. Circa 1983
            is a painting, a winter scene

like the one in which gray smoke rises
      from each chimney, flecked orange from fires

          that must be inside, unseen. The children
          are so small, they are faceless.

The Story of the Mountain

Home is not what the woman
had imagined. Late fall, the fields

are cropped to stubble, the mountain
already rust and smoke. The trees

must have flamed here but she's
too late. The man has threaded himself

through the trees on their best
black horse, and a hawk has dropped

its shadow on the child and won't
lift it away. The girl is learning to read

the world, and every turned page
reveals something peculiar, wholly new.

In the story of the mountain, the trees
burn for as long as they can bear it,

the horizon blurs and wobbles
like a heat mirage. The woman

doesn't know how the story ends.
Like the mountain, it has a shape,

but she's too close to see it whole.

ORIENTATION

Because you're new here, you need someone,
but I'm too busy trying to keep you
in the twentieth century a while longer,
feeding logs into the woodstove's glowing mouth
while, in a house just down the street,
someone programs a thermostat.
Twentieth century? Who am I kidding?
It was never safe. In this young country,
you can trace danger farther than you can
follow it, back to fire licking the walls of caves,
back to flint skinning the animal to its source.
Nothing predates danger. A hundred years ago,
Roosevelt Avenue was not this green
tunnel of London planes, only rows of saplings
planted by someone looking toward the future
where we now live, always looking forward
or back. The twentieth century didn't
keep me, but not for lack of trying.
I made it out alive. What can I say but stay
alive? You're new, and there's too much to learn.

You could never take a car to Greenland,

my daughter says. Unless the car could float.
Unless by car you mean boat. Unless the ocean
turned to ice and promised not to crack.
Unless Greenland floated over here,
having lifted its anchor. Unless we could row
our country there. Our whole continent
would have to come along, wouldn't it? Unless
we cut ourselves free. What kind of saw
could we use for that? What kind of oars
could deliver one country to another?
She asks, Why is Greenland called Greenland
if it's not green? Why is Iceland called
Iceland if it's greener than Greenland?
Unless it's a trick, a lie: the name Greenland
is an ad for Greenland. Who would go
promised nothing but ice? Who would cut
her home to pieces and row away for that?

At your age I wore a darkness

several sizes too big. It hung on me
like a mother's dress. Even now,

as we speak, I am stitching
a darkness you'll need to unravel,

unraveling another you'll need
to restitch. What can I give you

that you can keep? Once you asked,
Does the sky stop? It doesn't stop,

it just stops being one thing
and starts being another.

Sometimes we hold hands
and tip our heads way back

so the blue fills our whole field
of vision, so we feel like

we're in it. We don't stop,
we just stop being what we are

and start being what?
Where? What can I give you

to carry there? These shadows
of leaves—the lace in *solace*?

This soft, hand-me-down
darkness? What can I give you

that will be of use in your next life,
the one you will live without me?

Past

What is the past?

We needed a word for everything before.
See how my saying this is already there, and there
for good—no fishing it out of that deep water,
the deepest there is. The past is a tide that drags out
but won't return to shore: even your question
has been carried off. Look, you can see it floating.
Anything heavier settles unseen like wreckage
for a silver ribbon of fish to slip through.
The past is not all distant. We can stand at its edge,
watching the waves do the backbreaking work
of pulling, pulling away. From the shore, the past
seems to go on forever, because it does. We say
it was a different time, but all times are different.
This one, for instance. And again, this one.

Heart

A child of, say, six knows you're not the shape
she's learned to make by drawing half along a fold,
cutting, then opening. Where do you open?
Where do you carry your dead? There's no locket
for that—hinged, hanging on a chain that greens
your throat. And the dead inside you, don't you
hear them breathing? You must have a hole
they can press their gray lips to. If you open—
when you open—will we find them folded inside?
In what shape? I mean what cut shape is made
whole by opening? I mean besides the heart.

Stitches

Twice they opened me
and twice, after sewing me shut,

        they said the thread would dissolve,
        they said my body would dissolve

the thread. But see how frugal
I've become, saving every stitch

        for future alterations and repairs.
        Any woman with my blood

saves—is a saver. When given one
sheet of paper, my daughter

        cuts out the heart she wants
        and keeps the scraps for stars,

snowflakes, flowers. Twice
they cut babies from my body,

        but the body remains.
        See how nothing is wasted.

The more they cut, the more I have.

THE CROWS

The girl was not born on the mountain,
but she has witnessed enough births

to know she would rather be cut
from a long, unspooling roll of shadow

than pulled from another's body,
screaming and slick, an animal.

She chooses to believe the crows
scissored her into being,

furiously cutting her shape long
and lean with their sharp cries.

Where have they flown off to,
the ones who made her from nothing?

The girl can throw her voice so far,
no one will find it.

LET'S NOT BEGIN

Let's not begin the poem with *and*,
though it begins that way

in spirit: one in a long list of—
let's not call them grievances.

I'm trying to love the world,
I am, but is it too much

to ask for two parts bees
vibrating their cups of pollen,

humming a perfect *A* note,
to one part sting?

Worry and console, worry
and console: it's how I stay

in shape. See, I'm sweating.
Some nights my daughter cries,

I don't want to be in the dirt,
and this is what I call a workout.

My heart's galloping hell
and gone from the paddock—

I don't want to be in the dirt
because I'll miss you—

and there's no stopping me.
But let's not end

with the heart as horse,
fear-lathered, spooked deaf.

I'm trying, I am, for her.
If I list everything I love

about the world, and if the list
is long and heavy enough,

I can lift it over and over—
repetitions, they're called, *reps*—

to keep my heart on, to keep
the dirt off. Let's begin

with bees, and the hum,
and the honey singing

on my tongue, and the child
sleeping at last, *and, and, and*—

HOME-FREE

There's no rhyme for how high the corn should be
in September, but I can see it, and I'm telling you

it's up to my chest, maybe even my neck—
it's hard to tell from the road—and it's brown,

and judging by the sibilance when the wind
rubs the husks together, it must feel like paper.

I didn't see myself living among husks. I didn't
see myself here, not once I'd left my mother's

and father's house. Not Ohio, not *round on the ends,*
not *high in the middle,* not where some creeks

are called cricks. I always thought I would leave,
home-free, and go anywhere: land of silver

mesquite branches, land of dry riverbeds
with stones a horse could spark its hooves on.

Not here, not *knee-high by July,* not in *the heart
of it all,* not where some cricks are creeks:

Alum, Big Darby, Blacklick. I didn't see myself
raising children here, raising as if they could

levitate if we focused our attention. I didn't
see myself dying in my hometown, not a few

miles from where I was born, not surrounded
by my children, their feet planted on the ground.

I can see them. They'll say I entered and left
through the same door. They'll say I was always here.

Deer Field

My daughter wants to know where the deer are.
We used to see them across the street
from the airport's long-term parking lots,
before backhoes tore down the trees
and piled them in the grass. At the intersection
of Broad and James, I tell her all of this
was forest before we were born, and it was
full of deer, but they had to leave
when people cleared the land for buildings—
that gas station, that drug store—and roads,
like the one we're on now. She says
it makes her sad. The few bare trees left
are leafed with black birds, wings trembling
a little in the wind. The sky is a single sheet
of corrugated cloud—rippled but seamless
as if to prove it was not manufactured.
She doesn't ask what they are building
by the airport, in what we called Deer Field.
It doesn't matter. I have changed her.
I have given her the first in a long list
of disappointments, clearing away
a perfect, wild space in her to make room.

NEST

For nesting, the hawk gathers the girl's
long hair—glinting, caught in a low branch,

snagged on a clothesline. Soon he'll look
for her gold curls, almost transparent

in the light, and see strands the color of bark,
dull and dark and straight. Sycamores

shed their roughest skin to reveal
the color of milk. Is the girl like this,

becoming again and again what she was
when the hawk first spied her—young,

shining like a broken bit of mirror
on the ground? The hawk doesn't know

this is a human story, the girl's story
he is only a small part of. High in a pine

is a soft, blond nest of baby hair.

Size Equals Distance

I can't walk across the lawn to enlarge a starling
like a photograph preview: 4 x 6, 5 x 7, 8 x 10.
If I could, the bird would be the size of a man
by the time I'm close enough to hold it,
which is why I can't explain to my children
why airplanes look small in the air and big
at the airport, how people fit inside that toy,
how they don't shrink as they rise, then grow
as they near the ground. How can I explain
proximity sometimes but not always
transforms? Size and distance can't be set
on opposite sides of an equation, as if
when you see something grow, it's growing
because you're nearing it. Consider the man-bird.
Consider the baby I can't hold any closer
to make him grow. Consider all the things
I can't miniaturize by running from them.

HARROWING

This world is harrowing, harrowing,
all harrow, as if harrow were what
the world is made of, what we are
made of, as if harrow were strings
to be strummed, tendons and veins
to be strummed, as if harrow
could be snapped between the teeth,
the word one letter from the white meal
inside our bones, the meal we could make
of ourselves, harrow, two letters
from the bird who might strum
with its beak what the body is made of,
what the world is made of, and in that
strumming become the song.

Lullaby

The man has been gone so long,
his own child won't know him.

She and the woman, they must have
their own stories now, their own songs—

some for hauling wood and water,
others to sweeten the girl's sleep.

The wilderness is a strange place
to slumber, always the other-worldly

howl of something too close.
The man has been gone so long,

working over the mountain, maybe
his child's hair will be dark and wild

as feathers, her eyes more yellow,
hawk-eyes always spying birds

in the leaves. When he left, the girl
was moon-faced, her wispy curls

as gold as his long ago. But memory's
spell is always broken. The man knows

her curls will darken as his did,
like honey left too long in the jar.

WHERE HONEY COMES FROM

When my daughter drizzles gold
on her breakfast toast, I remind her

she's seen the bee men in our tree,
casting smoke like a spell until

the swarm thrums itself to sleep.
She's seen them wipe the air clean

with smoke, the way a hand smudges
chalk from a slate, erasing *danger*

written there, as if smoke revises
the story of the air until each page

reads *never fear, never fear.* Honey
is in the hive, forbidden lantern

lit on the inside, where it must be dark,
where it must always be. Honey

is sweetness and fear. I think
the bees have learned to embroider,

to stitch the sky with warnings
untouched by smoke. Buzzing

is the sound of bees perforating the air,
as if pulling thread through over

and over, though the thread too is air.

ROUGH AIR

When the pilot calls it *rough air*,
I think of a cat's tongue
as if the air itself were textured,
as if we could feel its sandpaper
licking our skin. I swallow
my ears open, and the silence
that is not silence at all fills them.
What I thought were graves
from this height are houses
in neat white rows. In the absence
of faith I resort to magical
thinking. I pray to my children,
which is to say I conjure them,
imagine holding them until
I can feel them in my arms.
Like a sign that dings on, lit:
Mother. Though motherhood
never kept anyone safe.
Just a week ago, an opera singer
held her baby on her lap
as a mountain chewed their plane
to bits. How is that possible?
Didn't the mountain see the baby?
Motherhood never kept anyone
safe, though it's no fault of mothers.

There is no such thing as safety—
only survival and the absence
of survival: a plane, a mountain,
a cockpit door that cannot
be opened. I am galloping inside
the cold white of this cloud,
no sound of hooves.
I have chewed my cheeks
bloody. I am trying so hard
to trust lift and thrust,
holding a note my daughter
wrote to her stuffed cheetah:
Hi Spots we will play Legos after school.
In other words, I love you,
I will come back. A child
is not a talisman. Neither am I,
I'm afraid. I am in the sky,
but do not pray to me.
I have no power here.

LEAVES

How do leaves fall off the trees and
how did God build this car?

The tree stops needing the leaves, so it lets go,
and people built this car. Someone must have told you
what God made without telling you everything
doesn't mean everything. There is light, and the light
is good, but some is stoppered inside bulbs
manufactured in Schaumberg: heirloom light,
the soft incandescence of last century. Even the sun
will burn out, rattling with bits of broken filament,
but not in your lifetime or your children's children's
children's. And what of the dark? You can build it
yourself, with your own two hands. Do you remember
covering your eyes to hide, believing you made
yourself invisible? On second thought, the leaves
must let go, or else the tree would keep them.

THE HUNTERS

The hunters are just passing through.
The three men stop to rest,

to dip their ladles in the cold creek,
and there are the woman

and the child. The girl wears
the shadow of a hawk, feathers

like a fine-printed fabric on her skin.
The men don't know what to make

of the bird, how it hovers above her
like a kite held up by an undercurrent.

On the hillside, the lit tents glow
like lanterns. The hunters wonder

if this place is real, if they will find
their way back here and see nothing

but trees—no girl, no hawk,
no woman, no metallic cold rusting

their tongues, no spell of these woods
to be broken. But tonight the men

are warm, fed, their coarse hair cut,
their horses heaped with furs,

and the woman wears firelight
on her face, the paper lace of the dark

flickering—a reminder of the soft,
bewitching world inside the world.

Parachute

Because a lie is not a lie if the teller
believes it, the way beautiful things

reassure us of the world's wholeness,
of our wholeness, is not quite a lie.

Beautiful things believe their own
narrative, the narrative that makes them

beautiful. I almost believed it
until the new mother strapped

her infant to her chest, opened
the eighth-floor window,

and jumped. My daughter tells me,
after her preschool field trip

to the Firefighter Museum,
about the elephant mask, its hose

like a trunk, and the video of a man
on fire being smothered in blankets.

She asks me if she knows anyone
who *got dead in a fire*, anyone who

got fired. When will I die? she asks.
When I was a child, I churched

my hands, I steepled my hands,
and all the people were inside,

each finger a man, a woman,
a child. *When I die, will you*

still love me? she asks. The mother
cracked on the pavement—

how did the baby live? Look,
he smiles and totters around

the apartment eight stories up.
Beautiful things reassure us

of the world's wholeness:
each child sliding down the pole

into the fire captain's arms.
But what's whole doesn't sell

itself as such: buy this whole apple,
this whole car. Live this whole life.

A lie is not a lie if the teller
believes it? Next time the man

in the video will not ignite.
The baby will open like a parachute.

IF ANYONE CAN SURVIVE,

it's the motherless children in my daughter's books,
orphaned or abandoned or garden-variety alone
with their chipped cups mined from the dump,
their day-old bread squirreled from the bakery,
their milk chilling in glass bottles behind
the waterfall so it doesn't sour. They've learned
to sew their own clothes from rags. They can tie
their own shoes, a sailor's knot, a tourniquet.
They can snare and skin a rabbit, strike rocks
into fire. Speaking of fire, where are their fathers?
At war, in jail, or fly-by-night—what matters
is the mothers, who must be dead for any rising
action to happen. Nothing is as freeing as grief.
Motherless children—what do they have to lose?
They're camped in the glacier-hollowed canyon,
whose ice melted millions of years ago. Even
the canyon where the motherless sleep is motherless:
an orphan is anything that outlives what made it.

STORYBOOK

Elsewhere in this world there is water
you cannot see beyond, the hunters say,

and seabirds. The men say the ocean
is not so far from here, and the more

they say it, the more the girl smells salt
on the piney air. Elsewhere in this world

is water you cannot cross on horseback
or raft, but here is all tinder and leaves,

all paper like a book cracked open
on its spine, and these mountains,

this intricate forest, cut from its pages.
The girl wonders if this is what the crows

have been doing with their sharp cries:
cutting leaf shapes from paper, cutting

their own shadows to throw down,
cutting the hawk's so it can follow her.

She wonders if when a baby is born
on the mountain, a caw cuts the child's

shape from flesh, too. The girl
could be elsewhere in this world, but here

she has a long, dark girl to lie down beside.

STONEFISH

There are fish in the black trenches
of the sea that look like rocks.
Their poison shouldn't trouble me.
They are so deep, we'll never touch.
But I think of them. If it is paranoid
to believe there is a trench in me
the doctors haven't dragged,
a cave no one's plumbed with light,
then fine, I'm paranoid. But whatever
plaques and tangles, whatever cells
wait deadly with their terrible hunger
must be disguised. You should know
the most venomous fish lives
in the shallows. It also looks like a rock.

ILLUSTRATION

Night was a secret
we kept from the children.

They had never seen it except
in picture books: the sky
ombre, blue at the roofs

gone indigo gone plum
gone black at the margins.

Stars impossibly star-shaped.
The moon flat and round.

When after dark they pressed
their palms to our windows,
the children saw only themselves.

If they thought of their hands
as five-pointed, they never let on.

How many dimensions
did we owe them? One more
than we gave. The only depth

they knew was depth of color.
The only moon they knew,
a white hole in the wallpaper.

The only stars, sharp-fingered
and near enough to pick at it.

The children weren't prepared
for the night they'd find, finally
stepping outside—the sky

wholly black, black root
to tip, the stars like freckles,
they marveled, no shape at all.

And the moon? The moon
was so new, it was missing.

INVINCIBLE

The babies made me invincible.
Even as they slept, they protected me.
Even as they slept, I could stomach the dark.
I could walk up the stairs, lights out,
and pass the mirror without hurrying.
I was divine, hovering inches above the floor
in a cloud sweet as milk—none of Therese's
rose perfume. I glowed with love but also
with suffering. Even the suffering
I wore like a blue robe, beautiful enough
for a painting. I felt the sky guarding me.
When I wore the babies and under
the babies the blue robe of my suffering,
I was lit from within. I burned myself
for fuel, shoveling black stones into
the stove inside me. The milk boiled
and grew skin. It turned. Still I felt nothing
could harm me—nothing would dare.
I was essential. I was too needed
in the world. That feeling was a spell
that is only now beginning to break.

Your Tongue

*That hawk is what
the wind says.*
—ARACELIS GIRMAY

Where is your voice now
that you have moved, you have migrated?

What has the land done to your tongue?

It is not dirt I hear in your crumbling mouth.
We did not bury you. When a tongue burns,

is it burned always? Does it hurt you?

I can't understand you, or you are not
speaking; there is nothing to say or

there is no way to say it. I wish you could

write to me. I miss your script.
Where is your voice? I know more or less

where your mouth is scattered,

where we scattered your mouth, but where
are your teeth, where is the gold in them?

SPLINTER

The man returns, beard thick and rough
as splintered wood, and finds what he feared:

the woman happy, the blond baby
he left now a dark-haired girl.

He knows hunters passed through;
the girl has a fox fur the color of rust.

The woman must have been lonely.
She must have worn her hair—the color

of a copper kettle—with one loose tendril
at the nape of her neck. The firelight

must have come alive on her skin.
Now she comes in alone from the pasture

at night, raised lantern swaying. She lies
a long time with the child, whisper-singing

some lullaby he's never heard into her hair.
This side of the mountain isn't home

anymore. In the morning, as the man splits
logs for the fire, a long splinter stitches

itself into the tender meat of his palm.
He dips his hand into the cold creek

and watches the water cloud with blood,
then run clear, as if he had never been there.

The Mother

The mother is a weapon you load
yourself into, little bullet.

The mother is glass through which
you see, in excruciating detail, yourself.

The mother is landscape.
See how she thinks of a tree
and fills a forest with the repeated thought.

Before the invention of cursive
the mother is manuscript.

The mother is sky.
See how she wears a shawl of starlings,
how she pulls it, thrumming, around her shoulders.

The mother is a prism.
The mother is a gun.

See how light passes through her.
See how she fires.

WHAT I CARRIED

I carried my fear of the world
to my children, but they refused it.

I carried my fear of the world
on my chest, where I once carried
my children, where some nights it slept
as newborns sleep, where it purred
but mostly growled, where it licked
sweat from my clavicles.

I carried my fear of the world
and apprenticed myself to the fear.

I carried my fear of the world
and it became my teacher.
I carried it, and it repaid me
by teaching me how to carry it.

I carried my fear of the world
the way an animal carries a kill in its jaws
but in reverse: I was the kill, the gift.
Whose feet would I be left at?

I carried my fear of the world
as if it could protect me from the world.

I carried my fear of the world
and for my children modeled marveling
at its beauty but keeping my hands still—
keeping my eyes on its mouth, its teeth.

I carried my fear of the world.
I stroked it or I did not dare to stroke it.

I carried my fear of the world
and it became my teacher.
It taught me how to keep quiet and still.

I carried my fear of the world
and my love for the world.
I carried my terrible awe.

I carried my fear of the world
without knowing how to set it down.

I carried my fear of the world
and let it nuzzle close to me,
and when it nipped, when it bit
down hard to taste me, part of me
shined: I had been right.

I carried my fear of the world
and it taught me I had been right.
I carried it and loved it
for making me right.

I carried my fear of the world
and it taught me how to carry it.

I carried my fear of the world
to my children and laid it down
at their feet, a kill, a gift.
Or I was laid at their feet.

Good Bones

Life is short, though I keep this from my children.
Life is short, and I've shortened mine
in a thousand delicious, ill-advised ways,
a thousand deliciously ill-advised ways
I'll keep from my children. The world is at least
fifty percent terrible, and that's a conservative
estimate, though I keep this from my children.
For every bird there is a stone thrown at a bird.
For every loved child, a child broken, bagged,
sunk in a lake. Life is short and the world
is at least half terrible, and for every kind
stranger, there is one who would break you,
though I keep this from my children. I am trying
to sell them the world. Any decent realtor,
walking you through a real shithole, chirps on
about good bones: This place could be beautiful,
right? You could make this place beautiful.

Transparent

The girl wonders: If she held a lantern
before the woman until she went

transparent enough to read through,
would she see the child inside

like a letter full of secrets? Once the girl
was part of the woman, tethered

inside her, transparent herself—
until the winter she writhed into air,

a new creature entirely. Darkness
inside the body must be woods-black.

The girl wonders: If she held a lantern
before the woman, would she see

what became of the unfinished child
bled away in the far field? She wonders

if its ghost is still on the mountain,
hovering birdlike in the scent

of the woman's hair. If the woman
went transparent enough, the girl

wonders if she would see a shadow
inside her, a small lobe of darkness

nestled beside the living child.

CLOCK

What kind of clockmaker
builds a clock inside a body.

What kind of clockmaker
builds a clock inside a body
then refuses to wind it.

What kind of clockmaker
winds a clock inside a body
then stops it.

What kind of body
holds a clock that refuses
winding.

What kind of body
holds a clock that is wound
but stops.

What kind of body
holds a clock that can't keep
the time.

What kind of clock
can't keep the time.

What kind of clock.

What kind of time.

FUTURE

What is the future?

Everything that hasn't happened yet, the future
is tomorrow and next year and when you're old
but also in a minute or two, when I'm through
answering. The future is nothing I imagined
as a child: no jet packs, no conveyor-belt sidewalks,
no bell-jarred cities at the bottom of the sea.
The trick of the future is that it's empty,
a cup before you pour the water. The future
is a waiting cup, and for all it knows, you'll fill it
with milk instead. You're thirsty. Every minute
carries you forward, conveys you, into a space
you fill. I mean the future will be full of you.
It's one step beyond the step you're taking now.
What you'll say next until you say it.

Cloud Study

Clouds, come down to sleep in the treetops—
if you've seen the pines' wide boughs

cradle the snow, even from a distance,
you know they can hold you. Or float

yourself into a roofless, falling-down barn
and lie in the moldering hay. So what

if the crows panic at the fallen sky, at the erased
horizon? They're suspicious, easily startled.

Let them blanket the ground, barking.
Let them spook the horses. The horses

will settle in the amnesia of darkness.
Clouds, come down. The end will be no

nearer than when you kept your distance—
nothing will keep you here. When you're ready

to rise again, you will. I can almost hear you
considering. If you want to lay your whiteness

in the field, if you want to steep in the lake
where you've watched your slow reflection cross,

come down. It will be like trying on glasses
for the first time. See, the hills aren't one

unbroken reach of green but pointillist,
millions of leaves—spades, spears, hands.

Clouds, have you seen me? I've cut my hair.
I have a new son. My boy mouths everything,

and he'd mouth you. Come be a cold discovery
dissolving on his tongue. Let me see you

up close, no longer godlike, not Constable's,
but sweet and slack as any face in sleep,

a clean page anyone could write on.

The Hawk-Kite

The boy watches the girl fly
the hawk above her, a kite of feathers

and flesh and bones. She must hold
an invisible string in her hand.

When she runs, the hawk-kite
sails with her. When she stands still

in the field, he hovers above her,
projecting his shape like an overlay

of feathers printed on her skin.
Wearing the black lace of its shadow

all her life has changed her. The boy
looks at her pale arms and sees wings.

Reading the Train Book, I Think of Lisa

In the board book there is a train, not a train
but a picture of a train on thick cardboard pages
my son fumbles to turn. In the book with a spine
gummed soft, there is no car parked beside the tracks
and no black-haired woman standing by the car
not parked beside the tracks. In the book
there is a train, each car its own color, one car
heaped high with coal, not coal but a drawing of coal.
See the engine, the neat cloud of steam above it,
not steam at all, and the engineer in his striped cap
smiling in the little window, not a window.
In the book there is no black-haired woman
on the tracks, not tracks. I am holding my son
who is holding the train book and waiting
for me to sing the long, happy sound, not happy
but a warning, doubled and doubled again.

PANEL VAN

You know the one about the white panel van,
the one about the dark sedan, the one I told
my daughter this morning,

the one about the man who's lost and needs
directions, the one about the man who lost
his puppy, the one that goes come here,

I'll show you a picture of my puppy,
the one that goes he's so cute, isn't he,
such a cute little lost puppy.

I told my daughter the one about the not-lost
not-puppy. I redacted the part about what's lost
being something in the man, something

he thinks a child can help him find, or maybe
he thinks she has it. She doesn't have it.
I didn't tell my daughter

the man was once a child. He had a mother
who zipped his tricky winter coat, tamed
his cowlick with her spit-wet thumb,

and how could she have known her son
would search the web for *cute puppy*
pictures, then roll past a park. This morning

I told my daughter the one about still loving
the world we live in, the world the man
lives in, lost. Yes, the same world.

POEM WITH A LINE FROM *BLUETS*

I could bury my face in it, *the sad sack of a town*
with hair that smells like an animal, bury my face
in its dark fur, wrap my arms around its barrel ribcage,
holding on for dear life. The town is wild but it might
let me near it, sad sack of a town, acre after acre
of tall grass I could bury my face in. I could lie
and listen to it snuffling beside me. For what should I save
my longing? Forget the afterlife, the aftertown:
there is no knowing what happens beyond this
sad animal, this sack of hair. Forget the golden future
beyond future. I want to see all of it here, all of it
through these eyes, in this animal body, while I am still
discernibly myself, while my shadow falls
on this sad sack of a town, this dear life.

Dear

you, you two, you who have me
in common—not-mother, mother

you weren't to have: Don't you
know each other, don't you live

in the air around me, *live*
being the perfectly wrong word?

Dear you, you dears, aren't you
together swimming the air,

buoyed by my son's breath
as he sleeps? You might slip

his ringlets like rings onto
your fingers if you'd had fingers.

I don't think you did. If I'd seen
inside myself, I'd have seen

what I could nearly hear:
a machine whirring, assembling

eyes, ears, limbs, rung by rung
of spine, then the grind

of metal-on-metal. Forgive me
whatever gear rusted and locked,

whatever spring sprung too soon.
It is always the same dream

but not a dream. Don't I feel you
treading the air around me

or what I feel is air rippling
in your wake, or is it wakes?

Dear you, you two—not-dears,
dears I was not to have—

if you swim, swim here.

MOUNTAIN CHILD

When the girl leaves the mountain
she is no longer a child

but she has not outgrown the hawk.
She wears its shadow on her shoulder,

an epaulet. It bears the weight
of allegory. When the girl leaves

the mountain, it's autumn,
so many yellow leaves on the gingko,

clusters of butterflies seem to cling
to each branch. Each time

the wind blows, a few take wing.
When the girl leaves, the mountain

flickers with shadows. What else
can left-behind birds offer

but their own shapes cut
from the papery dark. They call, *Please.*

The ground beneath her feet is a trick
of gold wings—at any moment a few

might flutter, then rise all at once.

Love Poem

What can I give you? You have plenty
of seas, seven at last count, and another

version of yourself beneath them, unseen:
doppelgänger caves and mountains,

the tallest secret ranges not for climbing.
Besides, I can't make you a sea

or fill each transparent wave with equally
transparent fish. I can't assemble

a forest or populate the trees with birds.
You have all the cranes you could want,

feathered or folded from paper. Look,
I have these two babies—but you?

You have more children than you can feed,
more than you can keep alive. Every day

you lose thousands, gain thousands.
No wonder the numbers mean nothing.

You need more than I or anyone can give.
But, fool that I am, I love you. I'm hot

for you. Here, warm your hands by the fire.
I made it with myself and a match.

RAIN, NEW YEAR'S EVE

The rain is a broken piano,
playing the same note over and over.

My five-year-old said that.
Already she knows loving the world

means loving the wobbles
you can't shim, the creaks you can't

oil silent—the jerry-rigged parts,
MacGyvered with twine and chewing gum.

Let me love the cold rain's plinking.
Let me love the world the way I love

my young son, not only when
he cups my face in his sticky hands,

but when, roughhousing,
he accidentally splits my lip.

Let me love the world like a mother.
Let me be tender when it lets me down.

Let me listen to the rain's one note
and hear a beginner's song.

Acknowledgments

Thanks to the editors of the following journals in which the following poems first appeared, sometimes in slightly different versions or with different titles:

32 Poems: "Love Poem" and "Transparent"

The Account: "Stonefish"

Alaska Quarterly Review: "Twentieth Century"

burntdistrict: "Harrowing"

Catamaran Literary Review: "London Plane"

diode: "First Fall," "Future," "Orientation," and "This Town"

The Georgia Review: "Cloud Study"

Guernica: "Let's Not Begin"

Hotel Amerika: "The Crows," "Leaves," and "Past"

Indiana Review: "Accidental Pastoral"

Kenyon Review Online: "Reading the Train Book, I Think of Lisa"

Linebreak: "Stitches"

Magma Poetry (UK): "Weep Up"

Nashville Review: "At your age I wore a darkness" and "Illustration"

The National Poetry Review: "Deer Field"

Pangyrus: "Invincible"

Pleiades: "Parachute"

Ploughshares: "Rough Air"

Plume: "Sky"

Redivider: "What I Carried"

Shenandoah: "Lullaby" and "The Story of the Mountain"

Southern Indiana Review: "Rain, New Year's Eve"

The Southern Review: "The Hawk," "The Hunters," "Marked," "Mountain Child," "Nest," "Splinter," "Storybook," and "You could never take a car to Greenland,"

Stirring: "Home-Free"

Sugar House Review: "Panel Van"

Thrush: "Clock," "Dear," and "Size Equals Distance"

Tinderbox: "Heart"

Virginia Quarterly Review: "The Hawk-Kite" and "Where Honey Comes From"

Waxwing: "Good Bones," "The Mother," and "Poem with a Line from *Bluets*"

The Well Review (Ireland): "If Anyone Can Survive" and "Museum"

Special thanks to Jessica Faust at *The Southern Review* for her spot-on edits on the poems that first appeared there.

Thank you to Natasha Trethewey for selecting "Good Bones" for inclusion in *The Best American Poetry 2017* (Scribner, 2017); to Amit Majmudar and Deborah Garrison for including this poem in *Resistance, Rebellion, Life: 50 Poems Now* (Knopf, 2017); to Speigel & Grau for including it in *How Lovely the Ruins: Inspirational Poems and Words for Difficult Times* (Spiegel & Grau, 2017); to the Poetry Foundation for e-mailing it to *Poem of the Day* subscribers; and to the Academy of American Poets for including "Good Bones" in the 2016 online anthology *Poems for After the Election*, with special thanks to Jen Benka for her friendship and support. Thank you to writer Joy Gregory and the cast and crew of the television drama *Madam Secretary* for featuring the poem on their episode "Good Bones," which aired on CBS on April 9, 2017. And thanks to Josef Beery, who designed and printed the limited-edition letterpress broadside of "Good Bones" available from Tupelo Press, and who also designed this book.

Gratitude also to Hannah Stephenson and the late Okla Elliott for reprinting "Marked" and "This Town" in *New Poetry from the Midwest 2014* (New American Press, 2015) and "Reading the Train Book, I Think of Lisa" and "Where Honey Comes From" in *New Poetry from the Midwest 2016* (New American Press, 2017). And thanks to Dante Di Stefano and María Isabel Alvarez for reprinting "What I Carried" in *Misrepresented People* (NYQ Books, 2017), and for donating all profits from the anthology to the National Immigration Law Center.

Thank you, too, to the editors at Magma Poetry for selecting "Weep Up" as the winner of the 2015–2016 Magma Poetry Editors' Prize.

I'm especially grateful to the National Endowment for the Arts, the Ohio Arts Council, and the Sustainable Arts Foundation for generous financial support, without which I would not have had the time—or childcare—necessary to write this book; to Stanley Plumly and Katie Pierce for their invaluable feedback on individual poems and on the manuscript as a whole; to artist Katherine Fahey, whose work inspired the hawk-and-girl poems, and to the Virginia Center for the Creative Arts for the residency fellowship that brought us together; to Jeffrey Levine, Marie Gauthier, Jim Schley, and all at Tupelo Press; to Jason, Violet, and Rhett, for this life that I love—with special thanks to Violet, whose thoughts and questions inspired many of these poems; and to my mother, Nita Smith.

OTHER BOOKS FROM TUPELO PRESS

Fasting for Ramadan (essays), Kazim Ali

Another English: Anglophone Poems from Around the World (anthology), edited by Catherine Barnett and Tiphanie Yanique

Personal Science (poems), Lillian-Yvonne Bertram

Everything Broken Up Dances (poems), James Byrne

Almost Human (poems), Thomas Centolella

Hammer with No Master (poems), René Char, translated by Nancy Naomi Carlson

New Cathay: Contemporary Chinese Poetry (anthology), edited by Ming Di

Rapture & the Big Bam (poems), Matt Donovan

Gossip and Metaphysics: Russian Modernist Poetry and Prose (anthology), edited by Katie Farris, Ilya Kaminsky, and Valzhyna Mort

Hallowed: New and Selected Poems, Patricia Fargnoli

Poverty Creek Journal (lyric memoir), Thomas Gardner

My Immaculate Assassin (novel), David Huddle

Darktown Follies (poems), Amaud Jamaul Johnson

Dancing in Odessa (poems), Ilya Kaminsky

A God in the House: Poets Talk About Faith (interviews), edited by Ilya Kaminsky and Katherine Towler

Third Voice (poems), Ruth Ellen Kocher

A Camouflage of Specimens and Garments (poems), Jennifer Militello

The Cowherd's Son (poems), Rajiv Mohabir

Marvels of the Invisible (poems), Jenny Molberg

Yes Thorn (poems), Amy Munson

Canto General: Song of the Americas (poems), Pablo Neruda, translated by Mariela Griffor and Jeffrey Levine

Lucky Fish (poems), Aimee Nezhukumatathil

Ex-Voto (poems), Adélia Prado, translated by Ellen Doré Watson

Why Don't We Say What We Mean? (essays), Lawrence Raab

Intimate: An American Family Photo Album (hybrid memoir), Paisley Rekdal

Thrill-Bent (novel), Jan Richman

The Voice of That Singing (poems), Juliet Rodeman

Walking Backwards (poems), Lee Sharkey

Wintering (poems), Megan Snyder-Camp

Service (poems), Grant Souders

Swallowing the Sea (essays), Lee Upton

See our complete list at www.tupelopress.org

Printed in the USA
CPSIA information can be obtained
at www.ICGtesting.com
BVHW041652160823
668591BV00004B/15